YOUR KNOWLEDGE HAS VALUE

- We will publish your bachelor's and master's thesis, essays and papers

- Your own eBook and book - sold worldwide in all relevant shops

- Earn money with each sale

Upload your text at www.GRIN.com and publish for free

Bibliographic information published by the German National Library:

The German National Library lists this publication in the National Bibliography; detailed bibliographic data are available on the Internet at http://dnb.dnb.de .

This book is copyright material and must not be copied, reproduced, transferred, distributed, leased, licensed or publicly performed or used in any way except as specifically permitted in writing by the publishers, as allowed under the terms and conditions under which it was purchased or as strictly permitted by applicable copyright law. Any unauthorized distribution or use of this text may be a direct infringement of the author s and publisher s rights and those responsible may be liable in law accordingly.

Imprint:

Copyright © 2017 GRIN Verlag, Open Publishing GmbH
Print and binding: Books on Demand GmbH, Norderstedt Germany
ISBN: 9783668523968

This book at GRIN:

http://www.grin.com/en/e-book/371086/distributed-denial-of-service-ddos-attacks-and-iot-security

Robert Joodat, Eric Wang

Distributed Denial of Service (DDOS) attacks and IoT Security

GRIN Publishing

GRIN - Your knowledge has value

Since its foundation in 1998, GRIN has specialized in publishing academic texts by students, college teachers and other academics as e-book and printed book. The website www.grin.com is an ideal platform for presenting term papers, final papers, scientific essays, dissertations and specialist books.

Visit us on the internet:

http://www.grin.com/

http://www.facebook.com/grincom

http://www.twitter.com/grin_com

Distributed Denial of Service (DDOS) attack and IoT Security.

(Mirai Botnet)
Robert Joodat
Eric Wang

Abstract

The purpose of this report investigates the present state of Internet of Things (IoT) devices. It highlights the current security issues of using IoT devices, and discuss its possible solutions to maximise security and minimise DDoS and cyberattacks.

The measures that needs to be considered to prevent attack on IoT devices from Mirai botnet has been highlighted, which include the use of cloudflare's orbit and other general security practices. Cloudflare's orbit allows manufactures to implement virtual patchs for vulnerabilities found in IoT devices until those vulnerabilities are fixed through software updates.

Introduction to Denial of Service

Denial of service attacks has been a threat on the internet starting as far back as when Robert Morris released his internet worm in 1988 (DDoSPedia 2017). The internet was in its infancy, and the result was a little more than an inconvenience. In the age of cyberspace and ubiquitous connectivity, online business depends upon accessible services, but denial of service becomes a much more serious issue, and once which can have devastating consequences.

In an assessment carried out by Kaspersky Labs in 2015, the cost of such an incident is between $52,000 and $444,000, as a result of the inability to carry out core business, loss of contracts and opportunities, credit rating impact, and insurance premium increases. This is significant enough to justify external testing to ensure the business is resilient (Kaspersky 2015).

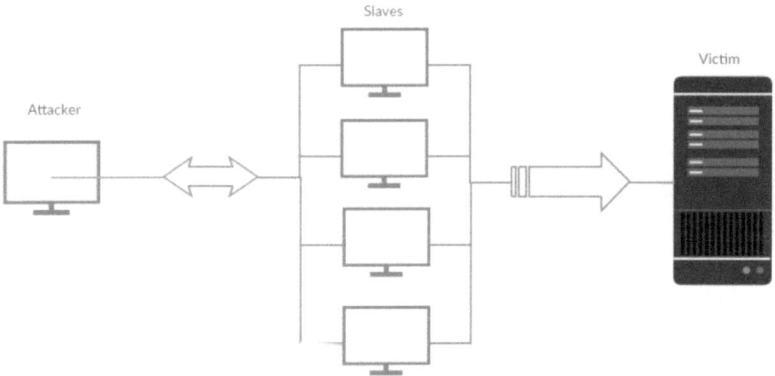

Figure 1: DDOS model

Denial of Service Attack Types

There are many different ways to achieve a denial of service, and it would take a very long time to enumerate them all. Denial of service is a name given to the class of cyber-attacks for which the aim is to destruct or deny use of a business service, be that a website, or some other service accessible from outside the organization. An attack might be from one source, in which case it is called simply, a denial of service.

The attack may be from multiple sources, in which case it is known as a distributed denial of service. This is more complicated because it firstly requires access to a large number of compromised systems, a botnet, which can be used as distributed sources, all controlled from one master attack workstation.

There are many attack techniques, which can be used to deny services, and these will result in one of three classes of impact. The first is Choking Access to the service, in which the pathway from the client to the service is overloaded or congested, in such a way as to make it difficult or impossible for a legitimate request to get through. The second is Disabling The Service, typically by sending a malformed packet which causes some form of internal malfunction in the service or application.

The third type of impact is Downgrading Service Performance, typically done by exhausting host resources for providing services. In addition to the three classes of attack, and the three types of impact, there are three classes of attack techniques. The first is network-based attack techniques, which depend on some form of protocol manipulation to exhaust resources. These include the following attacks. The TCP SYN flooding attack, which partially creates a TCP session, but does not complete the session handshake, and so consumes resources to maintain status information on the half-open connection.

The ICMP Smurf flooding attack: a reflective attack using the ICMP echo, because the source address is forged as the target address and the ICMP response is sent back to the target. If sufficient ICMP requests are made, the response packets flood the target's bandwidth. UDP flooding. A UDP flooding attack is just a distributed denial of service attack in which any form of UDP packet is sent to the target, and flooding occurs because, with a large number of emitting sources, the volume of packet data can easily exceed the target's incoming bandwidth.

ARP flooding: The ARP protocol is used in local area networks to identify the association between MAC address and IP addresses, so the internet routing can be done using MAC addresses. By corrupting the ARP caches and individual network hosts, these hosts can be isolated from the network, thus denying resources. The DNS amplification or reflection attack, a variant of the Smurf attack, this is another reflective attack in which a request is made to a DNS server, and the DNS response, which is over 50 times larger, is returned.

This leverages not only the number of responses but also their size, to congest the network. A similar approach can be achieved using the NTP service, gaining up to 50 times the amplification effect. A global NTP flooding attack took place in early 2014, causing hour-long outages in many data centres around the world (Cloudflare Blog 2014). The second class of attack is wireless network attacks. These often require the attack to be in close proximity to the wireless network and are focused on stopping workstations connecting.

These include the following attacks.

The de-authentication attack: The attack monitors for workstations trying to authenticate and issues a specific de-authentication request to that workstation. Alternatively, a broadcast de-authentication can be sent, which affects all workstation. The routing congestion attack, in which an adversary can flood the network by sending a large number of route requests, causing high levels of congestion, which, in turn, disrupts routing. The final class of attack techniques is known as application or host-based attack, which exploit vulnerabilities in the operating and application code on the target host.

This class of attack can exploit certain algorithms, memory structures, implementation specifics and so on. Each of these attacks is typically system inversion specific. One of the key application level attacks is HTTP flooding to create a denial of service. Similar to ICMP, the HTTP flooding attack sends a large number of HTTP messages to a web server, typically in a way that resources are held open by the request, and causes it to consume all its connections. Many other applications are also vulnerable to attack, and I'll cover FTP later in the course.

Session Initiation Protocol (SIP) services such, as VoIP are increasingly becoming a key target as internet voice becomes a major carrier for businesses. There are a number of techniques that can be used to protect against denial of service attacks. These are often ineffective due to a lack of testing prior to the incident, and either fail when used or are not used because of the risk of failure. They can be implemented as an in-house capability or used in the form of DOS mitigation as a service. Mitigation typically involved diagnosing an attack and discarding packets that are identified as part of the attack.

Internet of Things

The internet of things are the physical devices embedded with electronics, software, sensors, actuators and network connectivity that enable devices to collect and exchange data (Brown,2016) International Telecommunication Unit defined Internet of Things as the infrastructure of the information society. It allows physical devices access or control cross entire existing network infrastructure remotely, and more directly put the physical world into computer-base system improve efficiency accuracy and economic benefit in addition to reduce human intervention (ITU, 2016). The International Telecommunication Unit (ITU) is mentioned that Internet of Things influenced our physical world into computer-base; it changes routines of human being. In general, it has benefits in few fields such as natural disaster management, urban management and healthcare.

- NATURAL DISASTER MANAGEMENT

The internet of Things has ability to predict, with fine-accuracy, it allows responsible organisation to respond more quickly and rapidly management targeted evacuations such as detect mudslides, avalanches, earthquakes and other natural disasters.

- URBAN MANAGEMENT

The Internet of Things embedded to automatic traffic management has effectively governs the flow of traffic based on ever-changing conditions; parking application embedded internet that intelligently guide cars to open spots, eliminating wasted time and energy and dramatically cutting back on emissions (Brien,2014).

- HEALTHCARE

The wearable devices with internet can detect health problems of individual, before they even occur, and immediately connect emergency responders with detailed information and family members as need (Brien, 2014).

The ideas above apparently describe three components in the reality, and undeniable Internet of Things has more influence of access to information and the ability to utilize that information in meaningful and appropriate ways and improve that Internet of Things will play more important role in the future generations (Brien,2014).

IoT Security

- INTERNET OF INSECURE THINGS

IoT vulnerabilities
The internet-able devices are significantly increased any devices connected, such as medical devices PCs, and cars, some harmless such as fridge or printer that could any easy route into a network for a hacker. Even these internet-able devices may not prime targets to protect, they still could be route into a network for a hacker to access valuable data, or use together to cripple a network.

- THE CONNECTED WORKPLACE

The lack of security or malicious threats is increased by use hundreds and thousands of internet-connected devices. For example, printers can be connected in the workplace without any security updates and patches of laptops and mobile phones.
The key of organisations or enterprises are to have clear view of their IT estate is visibility. The Internet of Thing devices should be considered as endpoint such as computer, mobile and tablet and should be monitored to detect malicious threats. The organisations or enterprises should

control monitor, assess, and investigate all endpoints that any compromise can be quickly remediated (Kumbhar, 2017).

- IOT MANAGEMENT

There is no standard platform to leverage the development of IoT applications, which means that designers need to start from scratch with each new application. The Applied Science and Technology Research Institute (ASTRI) has developed the "IoT Management and Application Platform" (IMAP), which allows the connection of a local network of devices to the Internet, and provides remote management of devices and data through a simple and customisable web-based graphical user interface. The system supports several technological standards for communication between devices, web interfaces and network architecture. This means the system can be used on different platforms to support IoT devices.

Mirai IoT Botnet

Mirai (Future in Japanese) written in C programing language is a Linux based botnet malware, unlike Remaiten malware that uses brute force method to gain access to Linux based systems Mirai is capable of scanning the internet for any device that is listening to telnet, It then performs rainbow attack using a table of default username and passwords to logon on the device to gain administrative privileges and establish command and control channel with the device. Once vulnerable devices has been exploited, they will be used as part of botnet to perform Distributed Denial of Service Attacks.
The recent DDOS attack on Dyn DNS service provider that took down giant websites such as Twitter, Spotify and Github on Europe and North America was the largest of it kinds in history that was performed using IoT devices. Analysts indicate that more than 100,000 Mirai IoT botnet nodes were used with traffic reaching up to 1.2 Tbps.(Peter Loshin 2016). Future more security analysts mentioned: "We have a serious problem with the cyber insecurity of IoT devices and no real strategy to combat it," Fidler said. (Nicky Woolf 2016).
According to one of Mirai botnet commander, he was able to easily get over 300,000 victims at a time (Gallagher 2016). Ever since ISPs seems to be paying more attention to security by filtering encrypted and insecure protocols such as telnet.

With the rapid growth of IoT devices and security being one of the main concerns more than ever, such attacks could be potentially end up in loss of revenue for many companies especially now that Mirai source code has been publically released and any script kitty could use it.

What is a bot net?
A series of connected online devices including PCs, IP Cameras, mobile devices and smart home appliances that are infected and being controlled by malware over the internet. Users are often unaware of their system being infected, as infected devices will stay idle until they receive commands from their commander to start an attack. Attacks performed by an army of botnets are

often Distributed Denial of Service (DDOS) attacks to exhaust computing resources and make an online service unavailable. (Storm, 2017).

Solution (Cloudflare Orbit: A New Approach to IoT security)

The world is changing with the help of cheap and powerful connected chips powering billions of connected devices around the world. Everything from cars, home thermostats and wearables are coming online. And while these tiny chips unlock incredible potential, security stays as the top concern.

General security practices applies to IoT such as changing default username and passwords, use of complex passwords to mitigate risk of brute force and rainbow attacks, Auditing, defining user privileges, Whitelisting, use of Intrusion Detection System (IDS) and Intrusion Prevention System (IPS) to analyse abnormalities on the network, tune true false alarms to minimise risk of intrusions as well as user awareness to social engineering.

Cloudflare's Mutual Authentication (TLS Client Authentication) creates a secure connection between an IoT device and its origin. When a device attempts to establish a connection with its origin server, cloudflare validates the device certificate. If the device has a valid certificate, like having the correct key to enter the building, the device is able to establish a secure connection. If the device certificate is missing, expired, or invalid, the connection is revoked.

IoT Vs PC Security model

In PC world when a vulnerability is found, vendor releases a hotfix or patch where the end users are responsible to download and install it. These updates keep PC software secure. IoT devices are also required hotfixes and patches through software update but the PC security model cannot scale up to 22 billion devices, most of IoT manufacturers often do not invest in over the air (OTA) update mechanisms, which could potentially minimise the risk of zero day attacks. In the meantime, IoT consumers never think about having to update their internet connected Washing Machines. (Matthew Prince 2016)

Cloudflare Orbit solves this problem at the network level by enforcing secure authenticated connection between IoT devices and their origin server using TLS client authentication that creates a secure and encrypted connection between an IoT device and its origin server when a device attempt to establish a connection with its origin server, cloudflare validates the device's certificate.

Orbit allows device manufacturers to deploy virtual patches instantly to block vulnerabilities across all devices on the network simultaneously to block vulnerabilities in real time by keeping malicious requests from reaching the device. This will buy time for device manufacturers to work on a patch to keep their devices from leaking data or launching DDoS attacks. Finally yet importantly, Cloudflare Orbit delivers IoT firmware updates directly from the cache, resulting in reduced bandwidth costs. Furthermore, Cloudflare's compression and performance optimisations reduce data transmission resulting in lower power consumption and battery life. (Cloudflare.com/orbit 2017)

Cloudflare traditionally offers multiple data security options from IP verification to full cryptographic connection signing as well as content delivery network CDN, TLS, SSL and DDoS defence. Recently they have announced Orbit.

In other words, orbit works sort of like a VPN for IoT devices.
Instead of focusing on patches and updates on individual IoT devices, Orbit provides an encrypted tunnel by using Transport Layer Security (TLS) for IoT devices to access the internet.

The traffic to and from the IoT devices will pass through the cloudflare's global network where almost all of malicious traffic and IPs are well known. The idea is to patch the vulnerabilities once it is issued from the manufacture but until then if the product is experiencing an issue, manufactures can use cloudflare dashboard to respond in the cloud by implementing virtual patch or blocking connectivity from compromised units.
This architecture gives the product owners the advantage of having some protection while they wait for the manufacture to come out with an official fix.

MIRAI VS. ORBIT

As mentioned previously once the orbit has been implemented on IoT devices, the entire traffic to and from the device is passed through the cloudflare's global network where it detects the malicious traffic requests and blocks it.

Thus in the case of denial of service attacks, all malicious traffics will be terminated by performing request validation within cloudflare's network.

Technical and implementation

Cloudflare's Orbit solution works by acting as a firewall in between IoT devices and the internet.

At the moment there are no SDKs available to individuals to implement this solution on their own, therefore cloudflare orbit solutions have to be implemented and configured by manufactures end point.

Flowchart

Our provided solution to mitigate DDoS attacks are divided into two stages. The initial stage includes the essential general security practices and second stage includes the use of Cloudflare Orbit.

STAGE 1

The first step includes the necessity of changing the default username and passwords as mirai actively looks for devices using default credentials to gain access.
The second step starts by disabling unnecessary ports and services. SSH is prefered over telnet as telnet transmits data over the network with zero encryption and SSH uses x11 standards to encrypt data.
Third step of our proposed solution starts with de-escalating users privileges based on their roles. This step is imperative, If the user's account is compromised, the attacker's abilities are limited to what the users roles are.
Fourth step of general security practice introduces whitelisting. In context: specifying what applications or services are permitted to run on the system. Network monitoring also plays a big role in security by detecting abnormal activities on the network to prevent intrusions.

Once above steps are successfully completed, Cloudflare's Orbit can be implemented to achieve maximum security.

STAGE 2

The second stage of our solution is implementing Cloudflare Orbit.
The flowchart explains that the IoT device will use it assigned client certificate from manufacturer to authenticate itself to cloudflare's network. If the authentication was successful, the device is granted access to inbound and outbound traffic. If not the connection will be terminated.

Conclusion

In conclusion, with rapid growth in use of IoT devices, we find it essential to improvise more security practices for its users. The use of Mirai botnet to perform denial of service on IoT devices still is a major security issue. Cloudflare Orbit is introduced to create more secure authentication practices for future risks and mitigate these types of botnet attacks.

Additionally, Orbit allows manufacturers to implement virtual patches. This feature allows manufactures to work on software updates and minimise the risk on zero day attacks. With that being said, as of right now there are no SDKs available for individuals to implement and configure Orbit on their IoT devices, therefore Orbit has to be implemented on IoT devices from manufacturers end point.

Traditionally, in PC security model, Microsoft patches vulnerabilities within its monthly software updates; this method is not scalable for up to 22 billion IoT devices, as most manufactures do not invest in over the air update mechanism.

References:

SEAN GALLAGHER. 2016. How one rent-a-botnet army of cameras, DVRs caused Internet chaos, viewed 25 April 2017, < https://arstechnica.com/information-technology/2016/10/inside-the-machine-uprising-how-cameras-dvrs-took-down-parts-of-the-internet/>. .

Editorial Team. 2015. DDoS attack can cost a company more than $400,000, viewed 25 April 2017, <https://www.interneteverywhere.my/2015/01/ddos-attack-can-cost-a-company-more-than-400000/>.

Matthew Prince. 2014. Technical Details Behind a 400Gbps NTP Amplification DDoS Attack, viewed 25 April 2017, <https://blog.cloudflare.com/technical-details-behind-a-400gbps-ntp-amplification-ddos-attack/>.

Radware. 2014. Morris Worm, viewed 25 April 2017, <https://security.radware.com/ddos-knowledge-center/ddospedia/morris-worm/>.

Nicky Woolf. 2016. DDoS attack that disrupted internet was largest of its kind in history, experts say, viewed 4 May 2017, <https://www.theguardian.com/technology/2016/oct/26/ddos-attack-dyn-mirai-botnet>.

Peter Loshin. 2016. DDoS attack that disrupted internet was largest of its kind in history, experts say, viewed 6 May 2017 <http://searchsecurity.techtarget.com/news/450401962/Details-emerging-on-Dyn-DNS-DDoS-attack-Mirai-IoT-botnet>.

Keycdn. 2016. DDoS Attack, viewed 9 May 2017 <https://www.keycdn.com/support/ddos-attack/>.

John Graham-Cumming. 2014. Understanding and mitigating NTP-based DDoS attacks, 12 May 2017, <https://blog.cloudflare.com/understanding-and-mitigating-ntp-based-ddos-attacks/>.

Internet of Things Global Standards Initiative ITU, June, 2015, viewed 10 May 2017, < http://www.itu.int/en/ITU-T/gsi/iot/Pages/default.aspx>.

Brown, Eric,September 2016, "Who Needs the Internet of Things?", viewed 10 May 2017, <https://www.linux.com/news/who-needs-internet-things>.

Brendan O'Brien. 2014. Why the 'Internet of Things' Is Important, 12 May 2017, <http://insights.wired.com/profiles/blogs/why-the-internet-of-things-is-important#axzz4feoh63T9>.

Darlene Storm. 2017. New Mirai IoT variant launched 54-hour DDoS attack against a U.S. college, viewed 15 May 2017, <http://www.computerworld.com/article/3186175/security/new-mirai-iot-variant-launched-54-hour-ddos-attack-against-a-us-college.html>.

Sheetal Kumbhar. 2017. Monitoring IoT devices to detect malicious threats, viewed 15 May 2017, <https://www.iot-now.com/2017/02/28/59065-monitoring-iot-devices-detect-malicious-threats/>.

José Cardoso. 2016. Internet of Things (IoT) - Security Challenges and Possible Security Approaches, viewed 17 May 2017, <https://www.linkedin.com/pulse/internet-things-iot-security-challenges-possible-jos%C3%A9-cardoso>.

ResearchSEA. 2015. Managing the Internet of Things, 17 May 2017, <https://www.sciencedaily.com/releases/2015/05/150528082030.htm>.

The Windows Club. 2015. Dangers of Internet of Things – Security Issues, viewed 18 May 2017, <http://www.thewindowsclub.com/dangers-of-internet-of-things-security>.

Dani Grant. 2017. Introducing Cloudflare Orbit: A Private Network for IoT Devices, viewed 18 May 2017, viewed 18 May 2017, <https://blog.cloudflare.com/orbit/?utm_content=buffer39d2c&utm_medium=social&utm_source=facebook.com&utm_campaign=buffer>.

João José Costa Gondim, Robson de Oliveira Albuquerque, Anderson Clayton Alves Nascimento, Luis Javier García Villalba, and Tai-Hoon Kim. 2016. A Methodological Approach for Assessing Amplified Reflection Distributed Denial of Service on the Internet of Things, viewed 20 May 2017,< https://www.ncbi.nlm.nih.gov/pmc/articles/PMC5134514/>.

Caiming Liu, Yan Zhang, Huaqiang Zhang, CL,YZ,HZ, (2013). Ninth International Conference on Computational Intelligence and Security. In A Novel Approach to IoT Security Based on Immunology. Chengdu, 2013. Chengdu: 1. School of Information Science & Technology, Southwest Jiaotong University, Chengdu 610031, China. 771-775.

Kyoochun Lee. 2015. The Internet of Things (IoT): Applications, investments, and challenges for enterprises, viewed 20 May 2017, <http://www.sciencedirect.com/science/article/pii/S0007681315000373>.

Robbie Binnie, Colin McLean, Amar Seeam, Xavier Bellekens, "X-Secure: Protecting users from big bad wolves", *Emerging Technologies and Innovative Business Practices for the Transformation of Societies (EmergiTech) IEEE International Conference on*, pp. 158-161, 2016.

YOUR KNOWLEDGE HAS VALUE

- We will publish your bachelor's and master's thesis, essays and papers

- Your own eBook and book - sold worldwide in all relevant shops

- Earn money with each sale

Upload your text at www.GRIN.com
and publish for free